Instant Migration from Windows Server 2008 and 2008 R2 to 2012 How-to

A step-by-step guide to installing, configuring, and updating to Windows Server 2012

Santhosh Sivarajan

PUBLISHING

BIRMINGHAM - MUMBAI

Instant Migration from Windows Server 2008 and 2008 R2 to 2012 How-to

First published: January 2013

Production Reference: 1170113

Published by Packt Publishing Ltd.
Livery Place
35 Livery Street
Birmingham B3 2PB, UK.

ISBN 978-1-84968-744-7

www.packtpub.com

Credits

Author
Santhosh Sivarajan

Reviewers
Mike Kline
Jacek Swiatowiak

Acquisition Editor
Joanne Fitzpatrick

Commissioning Editors
Harsha Bharwani
Meeta Rajani

Technical Editor
Varun Pius Rodrigues

Project Coordinators
Shraddha Bagadia
Esha Thakker

Proofreader
Lauren Tobon

Graphics
Aditi Gajjar
Valentina D'silva

Production Coordinator
Melwyn D'sa

Cover Work
Melwyn D'sa

Cover Image
Conidon Miranda

About the Author

Santhosh Sivarajan is a recognized subject matter expert in the Microsoft technology arena. He has extensive experience in designing, migrating, developing, and implementing enterprise solutions using Microsoft products and technologies. His certifications include MCITP, MCTS, MCSE, MCSA, Network+, CCNA, and many more. He is also a certified migration expert in Quest Migration Manager products.

His blog (`http://blogs.sivarajan.com`) and SS Technology Forum (`http://www.sivarajan.com/forum`) are well known in the industry for providing free technical information and support.

Microsoft has recognized Santhosh with the Microsoft Most Valuable Professional (MVP) award multiple times for his exceptional contribution to the technical community. He lives in Sugarland, Texas with his wife Anjali and daughter Gayathri.

First and foremost, I would like to thank God for giving me the power to believe in myself and to pursue my dreams.

Of course, I could not have completed this book without the support and encouragement from my family, especially my wife Anjali and my daughter Gayathri for giving up some of our time together so that I could share my ideas through this book.

I am also grateful to all my friends and colleagues for their support throughout my career. A special thanks for my MVP friends for listening to and supporting my ideas.

I would also like to express my special gratitude and thanks to the entire Packt Publishing team for this opportunity and their support throughout this process.

About the Reviewers

Mike Kline is an IT professional based in the Washington, D.C. area. After serving in the Army (97B) and attending George Mason University, Mike officially joined the IT industry in 1998, starting as a help desk technician and working his way up to his current role as a systems engineer working for SE Solutions Inc. Mike has supported numerous federal agencies.

He is a four-time Microsoft MVP awardee for Directory Services and holds several certifications, including MCSE, MCITP, MCSA Windows 2012, and CISSP. He's also active on several forums and has a personal blog at ADisfun.com.

I would like to thank all the great people I've worked with and MVPs and others that I've learned from over the years. Joe Richards, Dean Wells, Ned Pyle, and Laura Hunter are a few that stand out but there are many more, so thanks to everyone. I'd like to thank the geek/nerd squad: thanks Eric, Mark, Florian, Rich, Tad, and Troy. Thanks Richard G. and Gus C. for being the best bosses I've ever had. I'd like to thank my girlfriend Michelle for all her support and, last but not least, my brother Andy who has always been there through good and bad times.

Jacek Swiatowiak is a Polish MVP (in the years 2010-2012 for Forefront Family and since October 2012 for Directory Services). He has been a Microsoft Certified Trainer (MCT) since 2006 and also a MCSE 2003/Messaging/Security, 23 MCTS, 9 MCITP, MSA in Office Communications Server 2007 – U.C. Voice. He is a lecturer at Gdansk University of Technology (Faculty of Electronics, Telecommunications and Informatics) and Polish-Japanese Institute of Information Technology. He has 16 years of experience in designing and deploying Active Directory environments, focusing now on Microsoft's unified communication solutions. He has many publications on the Polish Microsoft TechNet website and other portals.

He is also an author of a book describing Microsoft Forefront Family. Currently he is working with other Exchange Polish MVP's on a book presenting Exchange 2013 and Lync 2013.

www.PacktPub.com

Support files, eBooks, discount offers and more

You might want to visit www.PacktPub.com for support files and downloads related to your book.

Did you know that Packt offers eBook versions of every book published, with PDF and ePub files available? You can upgrade to the eBook version at www.PacktPub.com and as a print book customer, you are entitled to a discount on the eBook copy. Get in touch with us at service@ packtpub.com for more details.

At www.PacktPub.com, you can also read a collection of free technical articles, sign up for a range of free newsletters and receive exclusive discounts and offers on Packt books and eBooks.

http://PacktLib.PacktPub.com

Do you need instant solutions to your IT questions? PacktLib is Packt's online digital book library. Here, you can access, read and search across Packt's entire library of books.

Why Subscribe?

- ► Fully searchable across every book published by Packt
- ► Copy and paste, print and bookmark content
- ► On demand and accessible via web browser

Free Access for Packt account holders

If you have an account with Packt at www.PacktPub.com, you can use this to access PacktLib today and view nine entirely free books. Simply use your login credentials for immediate access.

Instant Updates on New Packt Books

Get notified! Find out when new books are published by following @PacktEnterprise on Twitter, or the *Packt Enterprise* Facebook page.

Table of Contents

Preface

Welcome to *Instant Migration from Windows Server 2008 and 2008 R2 to 2012 How-to*.

Microsoft Windows Server 2012 is the latest release of the server operating system from Microsoft. In this release, Microsoft has incorporated various enhancements to the existing functionalities and also introduced new features to support modern IT work environments and workload, which makes this operating system different from the other operating systems that Microsoft has released till date.

The book will walk you through different migration and deployment scenarios based on the author's real-world experience. The goal is to have a native Windows Server 2012 environment by the end of this journey.

To achieve this goal, this book is divided into multiple sections with several recipes. Each recipe will provide you step-by-step instructions for the migration of existing services onto a Windows Server 2012 environment as well as for decommissioning the old Windows Server 2008 or Windows Server 2008 R2 server from the current environment.

For a Windows Server 2008 and Windows Server 2008 R2 administrator, this book can be used as a reference manual when performing an upgrade or a migration.

What this book covers

Installing Windows Server 2012 (Must know), provides step-by-step instructions on installing Windows Server 2012 Server Core, Windows Server 2012 Server with a GUI, and Server Core to Server with a GUI and vice versa.

Converting Server Core to Server with a GUI (Should know), introduces methods using Windows PowerShell for converting Windows Server 2012 Server Core into Windows Server 2012 Server with a GUI.

Converting Server with a GUI to Server Core (Should know), provides methods using Windows PowerShell for converting a Windows Server 2012 Server with a GUI into Windows Server 2012 Server Core. This recipe also provides a method for identifying different types of Windows Server 2012.

Configuring Windows Server 2012 (Must know), provides an overview of Window Server 2012 Server Manager, performing administration tasks such as changing the computer name, joining a computer to a domain, and so on using Server Manager. It is also provides the details of administering a Windows Server 2012 Server Core using sconfig utility.

Installing administration tools (Must know), explains the details of installing Remote Server Administration Tools and new features available in Windows Server 2012 for managing and administering remote or local servers. This recipe also covers some of the deployment tasks that are relevant for migrating Windows Server 2008/R2 to Windows Server 2012.

Working with Server Manager properties (Should know), introduces the Server Manager dashboard and its capabilities for an administrator to efficiently manage the servers. This recipe also provides the details and capabilities of new Server Manager.

Adding servers to Server Manager (Should know), describes how multiple servers can be managed from the Server Manager dashboard and explains the details of adding a server to Server Manager from Active Directory, DNS, and using an import file.

Creating a server group (Should know), introduces the new server group concept, from where you can now manage and administer local and remote servers based on roles, features, or custom categories. This recipe provides step-by-step instructions on creating, managing, and modifying the group.

Enabling remote desktop (Should know), describes the new Server Manager's capabilities of remotely managing multiple servers. In certain instances, the administrators have to remotely log in to these servers using remote desktop connection. This recipe provides details of enabling and disabling remote desktop options.

Add and remove roles and features (Must know), introduces additional roles and features which can be deployed onto local or remote machines using the new Server Manager. In this recipe, we will explain a procedure to remove roles and features.

Active Directory migration (Must know), provides the details of Active Directory migration prerequisites, schema upgrade procedure, verifying the schema version, and installing the Windows Server 2012 Domain Controller in the existing Windows Server 2008 and Server 2008 R2 domain.

FSMO role transfer/migration (Must know), introduces some of the features of Windows Server 2012 that are only available when the FSMO role is running on the Windows Server 2012 Domain Controller. This recipe provides the details of these new features and also provides step-by-step instructions on transferring FSMO roles using PowerShell cmdlet and Windows Server Administration Tools.

Windows Server Migration Tools (Must know), provides you an overview of Windows Sever Migration Tools, PowerShell cmdlets details, installation instructions, and step-by-step instructions on creating an installation package for different types of servers.

Dynamic Host Configuration Protocol (DHCP) migration (Must know), explains the procedure for migrating DHCP scope and lease information using Windows Server Migration Tools.

DNS migration (Should know), provides the details of different types of DNS zones, zone replication details, and migration zones using secondary to primary conversion method and the `dnscmd` command.

Data and file server migration (Must know), describes how the file server or data migration can be achieved by migrating the data from the existing server onto a new server. In this recipe, I will be explaining a migration procedure using Windows Server Migration Tools cmdlet such as `Send-SmigServerData` and `Receive-SmigServerData`.

Printer and print server migration (Must know), provides details of migrating printers and associating its properties using the Print Management console. This recipe also provides instructions on installing Print and Document Services role onto Windows Server 2012.

Hyper-V migration (Should know), explains a couple of procedures for migrating Hyper-V guest machines from Windows Server 2008 and Windows Server 2008 R2 to a new Windows Server 2012 Hyper-V server.

Decommissioning old domain controllers (Must know), provides step-by-step instructions on uninstalling an existing Windows Server 2008 and 2008 R2 Domain Controller.

Forest and domain functional level (Must know), introduces some of the new Windows Server 2012 features that will only be available when the forest or domain functional level is set to a certain state. This recipe provides details of these new features, raising and lowering domain and forest functional levels, and verifying the functional level using directory services commands.

What you need for this book

As an administrator performing the migration, you need to have the Windows Server 2012 operating system at hand. You will also need to have the following software with you:

- Windows Server Migration Tools
- Windows PowerShell
- Remote Server Administration Tools

Who this book is for

The book is for server administrators who are responsible for the administration of Windows Server 2012 and performing migrations from their existing Windows Server 2008 / 2008 R2 environment to Windows Server 2012.

Conventions

In this book, you will find a number of styles of text that distinguish between different kinds of information. Here are some examples of these styles and an explanation of their meaning.

Code words in text are shown as follows: "`Server-Gui-Mgmt` can also be used to install additional features on a server."

Any command-line input or output is written as follows:

```
Move-ADDirectoryServerOperationMasterRole -Identity
"DCName" -OperationMasterRole SchemaMaste,
DomainNamingMaster,PDCEmulator,RIDMaster,InfrastructureMaster
```

New terms and **important words** are shown in bold. Words that you see on the screen, in menus or dialog boxes for example, appear in the text like this: "clicking the **Next** button moves you to the next screen."

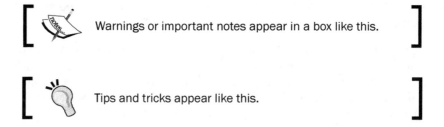

Warnings or important notes appear in a box like this.

Tips and tricks appear like this.

Reader feedback

Feedback from our readers is always welcome. Let us know what you think about this book—what you liked or may have disliked. Reader feedback is important for us to develop titles that you really get the most out of.

To send us general feedback, simply send an e-mail to `feedback@packtpub.com`, and mention the book title via the subject of your message.

If there is a book that you need and would like to see us publish, please send us a note in the **SUGGEST A TITLE** form on `www.packtpub.com` or e-mail `suggest@packtpub.com`.

If there is a topic that you have expertise in and you are interested in either writing or contributing to a book, see our author guide on `www.packtpub.com/authors`.

Customer support

Now that you are the proud owner of a Packt book, we have a number of things to help you get the most from your purchase.

Downloading the example code

You can download the example code files for all Packt books you have purchased from your account at http://www.PacktPub.com. If you purchased this book elsewhere, you can visit http://www.PacktPub.com/support and register to have the files e-mailed directly to you.

Errata

Although we have taken every care to ensure the accuracy of our content, mistakes do happen. If you find a mistake in one of our books—maybe a mistake in the text or the code—we would be grateful if you would report this to us. By doing so, you can save other readers from frustration and help us improve subsequent versions of this book. If you find any errata, please report them by visiting http://www.packtpub.com/support, selecting your book, clicking on the **errata submission form** link, and entering the details of your errata. Once your errata are verified, your submission will be accepted and the errata will be uploaded on our website, or added to any list of existing errata, under the Errata section of that title. Any existing errata can be viewed by selecting your title from http://www.packtpub.com/support.

Piracy

Piracy of copyright material on the Internet is an ongoing problem across all media. At Packt, we take the protection of our copyright and licenses very seriously. If you come across any illegal copies of our works, in any form, on the Internet, please provide us with the location address or website name immediately so that we can pursue a remedy.

Please contact us at copyright@packtpub.com with a link to the suspected pirated material.

We appreciate your help in protecting our authors, and our ability to bring you valuable content.

Questions

You can contact us at questions@packtpub.com if you are having a problem with any aspect of the book, and we will do our best to address it.

Instant Migration from Windows Server 2008 and 2008 R2 to 2012 How-to

This book is intended to serve as a hands-on reference manual for Windows Server administrators who are performing migrations from their existing Windows Server 2008 / 2008 R2 environment to Windows Server 2012. In this book, we provide you with many "how-to" deployment, migration, and administration scenarios. We will also walk you through different scenarios of installing, configuring, and migrating Windows Server 2012 in a real-world environment.

There are many ways to upgrade the current environment to a Windows Server 2012 environment. The in-place upgrade and migration are two key approaches. The **in-place upgrade** refers to the upgrade of your current server to a new state or operating system without reinstalling or reconfiguring the software or hardware components. The **migration** approach introduces a new server or operating system on a new hardware platform, and moves/migrates all existing resources into the new server. Both of these options have pros and cons. If you are performing an in-place upgrade, you need to make sure all the hardware, software, and applications support the new operating system. Microsoft Windows Server 2012 is only available in 64-bit. Since the in-place upgrade does not provide you with an option to select the components or the data you need to migrate, this process is often called the garbage-in and garbage-out method. The migration scenario involves more processes than just upgrading the operating system. It requires an actual migration process for all existing resources in the environment. It also requires additional hardware which can lead to more operational and maintenance costs during the migration or coexistence period. If a business can afford the cost of the new hardware, the migration approach is a safer and cleaner method than performing an in-place upgrade.

The focus of this book is on the migration approach. It provides a step-by-step instruction on migrating the existing services into a new Windows Server 2012 environment using native tools available on Windows Server 2012. The flow of the book is to provide you the administration and deployment details first, and then the migration details of various services. The goal is to have a complete Windows Server 2012 environment after the migration. This can be achieved by migrating the existing Active Directory domain, network services, file and print servers, and many more onto a Windows Server 2012 server.

The following figure graphically represents the high-level tasks involved in this migration process:

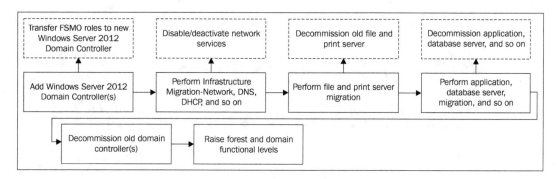

All these details and step-by-step instructions are included in the various recipes of this book in the following order:

- ▸ Windows Server 2012 Core and GUI installation and configuration
- ▸ Windows Server 2012 local and remote administration
- ▸ Active Directory and domain controller migration
- ▸ Network Services (DNS and DHCP) migration
- ▸ Data and file server migration
- ▸ Printer and print server migration
- ▸ Hyper-V and virtual server migration
- ▸ Decommissioning old servers and domain controllers

The installation and configuration sections ensure that the new Windows Server 2012 is functional and configured correctly. The migration sections provide you the details of migrating existing services into the previously configured server. The *Decommissioning old domain controllers (Must know)* recipe provides the details of decommissioning old servers and bringing the current infrastructure into a native Windows Server 2012 environment.

Installing Windows Server 2012 (Must know)

Now it is time to start installing servers in your environment. In this recipe, we will start installing Windows Server 2012 in Server Core and later it will be converted to a Server with a GUI. We will cover the following:

▶ Installing Windows Server 2012 with Server Core option

▶ Converting from Server Core to Server with a GUI and vice versa

▶ Basic configuration tasks

Getting ready

Windows Server 2012 is only available as a 64-bit version. So the hardware needs to support this requirement. The following is the minimum hardware requirement for Windows Server 2012:

▶ **Processor**: 1.4 GHz 64-bit processor

▶ **RAM**: 512 MB

▶ **Hard disk**: 32 GB

You also need to select the correct edition (Data Center, Standard, Essential, or Foundation) of the server based on your business and technical requirements.

The preceding hardware requirement is an absolute minimum requirement to install Windows Server 2012. The actual hardware and software requirements will vary based on the environment and the types of application you are going to support. It is recommended to perform a capacity planning session with various team owners before you finalize the hardware and server edition. Upgrade from the same server edition of Windows Server 2008 and Windows Server 2008 R2 to Windows Server 2012 is supported. Also, the Essentials and Foundation versions of Windows Server 2012 are on a separate install DVD.

How to do it...

1. Boot the server from the Windows Server 2012 CD.

2. Like other operating system (OS) installations, in the first screen you will see an option to select **Language to Install**, **Time and Currency Format**, and **Keyboard of input method**. Select the correct options based on your region. Click on **Next**.

3. Click on **Install Now** in the next window to continue the installation.

4. As shown in the following screenshot, you will see the **Server Core Installation** and **Server with a GUI** options. For this installation, I will select **Server Core Installation**. Click on **Next**.

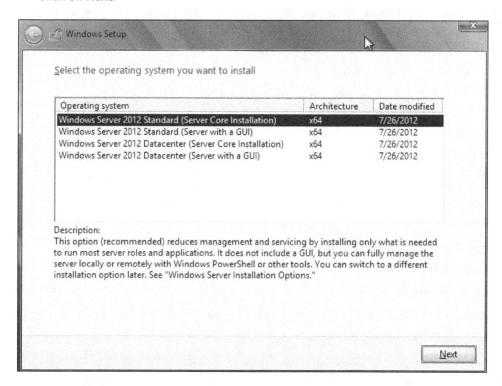

5. Accept the license agreement. Click on **Next**.

6. Since this is a new installation, you need to select the **Custom: Install Windows Only (advanced)** option. For an upgrade, select the **Upgrade: Install Windows and keep files, settings, and applications** option. Click on **Next**.

7. Select the drive where you want to install the operating system. Click on **Next**.

 Use the advanced option to format the drive, change the partition size, load drivers, and so on.

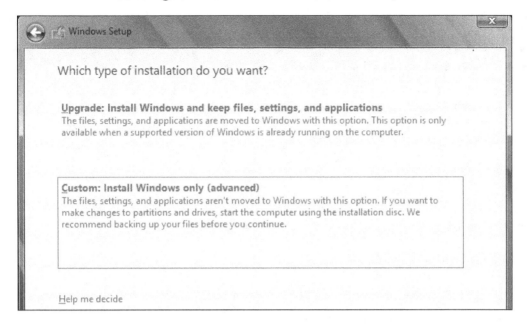

 You can use the left arrow button on the top-left corner of the screen to go back to the previous install screen.

8. Select the drive where you want to install the operating system. Click on **Next**. The installation process will start at this point. The installation process is categorized into five different stages: **Copying Windows Files**, **Getting files ready for installation**, **Installing features**, **Installing updates**, and **Finishing up**.

9. The server will be rebooted after the initial installation. After the reboot, the server will prompt you to enter a password for the built-in Administrator account. Enter a new password and click on **OK** to complete the installation.

How it works...

As I mentioned before, the default install option is Server Core. The previously mentioned procedure completes the installation of Windows Server 2012. At this point this server will be a standalone server.

There's more...

In Windows Server 2012, you can use the Setres (Set Resolution) command to change the default command windows resolution. Now you have completed the installation of a Server Core operating system (OS). Before we start configuring this server, I will explain the process of converting this server into a Server with a GUI option.

Converting Server Core to Server with a GUI (Should know)

You have a few options using PowerShell, Server Manager, Deployment Image Servicing and Management (DISM) tool, and a few others to convert a Server Core into Server with a GUI and vice versa. In this book I will be explaining a procedure using Windows PowerShell. The following recipe explains these details.

Getting ready

The minimum hardware and software requirements for a Server with a GUI is the same as a Server Core, which is described in the previous recipe.

How to do it...

1. Log on to the Windows Server 2012 core server with administrative credentials.
2. Start the PowerShell console from the command window by typing the command `PowerShell`.
3. From the PowerShell prompt, enter `Install-WindowsFeature Server-Gui-Mgmt-Infra, Server-Gui-Shell -Restart`.

[You can install multiple features in a single command line by separating these features by a comma.]

```
Administrator: Windows PowerShell                                  _ □ ✕
PS C:\> Install-WindowsFeature Server-Gui-Mgmt-Infra, Server-Gui-Shell -Restart

Start Installation...
     24%
     [oooooooooooooooo                                              ]
```

How it works...

The `Install-WindowsFeature Server-Gui-Mgmt-Infra, Server-Gui-Shell` cmdlet installs Server-Gui-Mgmt-Infra and Server-Gui-Shell Windows features on the Server Core. The `-Restart` parameter will force to reboot the server after the installation. After the reboot the server will be converted to a Server with a GUI.

There's more...

In the preceding procedure, we were using Windows Update as the source instead of a **Windows Imaging File** (**WIM**). Alternately, you can mount the WIM file locally to install additional features without accessing the Windows Update Service by using the `-Source` parameter in the previous cmdlet.

Converting Server with a GUI to Server Core (Should know)

This recipe explains the procedure to convert the Server with a GUI into Server Core using a PowerShell cmdlet.

Getting ready

The minimum hardware and software requirements for a Server with a GUI is the same as a Server Core which is described in the previous recipe.

How to do it...

1. Log on to the Windows Server 2012 server with administrative credentials.
2. Start the PowerShell console from the command window by typing the command `PowerShell`.
3. From the PowerShell prompt, enter the `Uninstall-WindowsFeature Server-Gui-Mgmt-Infra -restart` cmdlet.
4. Restart the server.

How it works...

The preceding process uninstalls the Server-Gui-Mgmt-Infra feature and the associated components from the server. If you are not sure which components will be affected by this cmdlet, you can use the `-whatif` parameter with the previous command.

As you can see in the following screenshot, if we use the previous command, it will remove **Graphical Management Tools and Infrastructure**, **Server Graphical Shell**, **User Interfaces and Infrastructure**, and **Windows PowerShell ISE**.

```
PS C:\> Uninstall-WindowsFeature server-gui-mgmt-infra -whatif
What if: Continue with removal?
What if: Performing uninstallation for "[User Interfaces and Infrastructure] Graphical Management Tools and Infrastructure".
What if: Performing uninstallation for "[User Interfaces and Infrastructure] Server Graphical Shell".
What if: Performing uninstallation for "[User Interfaces and Infrastructure] User Interfaces and Infrastructure".
What if: Performing uninstallation for "[Windows PowerShell] Windows PowerShell ISE".
What if: The target server may need to be restarted after the removal completes.

Success Restart Needed Exit Code    Feature Result
------- -------------- ---------    --------------
True    Maybe          Success      {Graphical Management Tools and Infrastruc...
```

You can specify a `-Remove` option with the preceding command to remove the installation binaries from the hard drive (disabled with payload removed). If you don't specify the `-Remove` option, the installation binaries will remain in the Windows Side-by-Side (`WinSxS`) folder. It can be used for future use without using an installation media or getting it from Windows Update.

There's more...

You can verify the installation type by validating the `ServerCore`, `ServerCoreExtended`, `Server-Gui-Mgmt`, and `Server-Gui-Shell` registry values in the `HKEY_LOCAL_MACHINES\SOFTWARE\Microsoft\WindowsNT\CurrentVersion\Server\ServerLevels` registry hives. These registry keys will be added based on the features installed on the server.

A Windows Server with a GUI will have `ServerCore`, `ServerCoreExtended`, `Server-Gui-Mgmt`, and `Server-Gui-Shell` registry keys as shown in the following screenshot. The Server Core will only contain the `ServerCore` registry key.

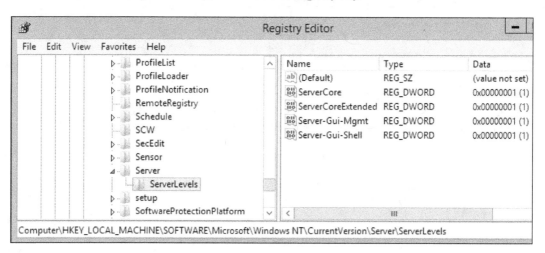

You can also use Server Manager from a local or remote machine to add or remove a feature on a server. The **Deployment Image Servicing and Management** (**DISM**) command `Enable-WindowsOptionalFeature –online -Featurename ServerCore-FullServer, Server-Gui-Shell, Server-Gui-Mgmt` can also be used to install additional features on a server.

Configuring Windows Server 2012 (Must know)

After the initial server installation, you need to configure the server with correct IP address, name, and so on before you start deploying new roles onto this server. Most of these components can be configured using Control Panel or Server Manager, which can be directly opened from the Start window of the server. As an Administrator, you need to get familiarized with the new Start window and Server Manager, so I would recommend you to configure these tasks using these options.

Getting ready

The following are some of the recommended administrative tasks which you can include in your server configuration checklist:

- ▶ Configure a static IP address, disable used network card, and so on
- ▶ Rename the default computer name
- ▶ Change/validate the time zone
- ▶ Activate the operating system
- ▶ Install updates and patches
- ▶ Install an antivirus software
- ▶ Enable RDP/remote administration options
- ▶ Join the computer to the domain

 Some of these tasks can be automated through domain/Group Policy Objects or some other deployment mechanism.

The configuration options for the Server Core are the same as in Windows Server 2008 and Windows Sever 2008 R2.

How to do it...

1. Log on to Windows Server 2012 Server with a GUI with administrative credentials.

2. From the Start screen select **Control Panel**. As you can see in the following screenshot, most of these components can be configured using Control Panel.

 Joining a Windows Server 2012 to your existing domain doesn't require an Active Directory Schema upgrade. However, you need to upgrade the schema if you are planning to add Windows Server 2012 as a domain controller. You will see these details in the *Active Directory migration (Must know)* recipe of this book.

3. The computer name and IP Address can be changed from Server Manager as shown in the following screenshot:

    i.   From **Server Manager**, select **Local Server** in the left node.

    ii.   Change the **Name**, **Workgroup**, and so on from this window.

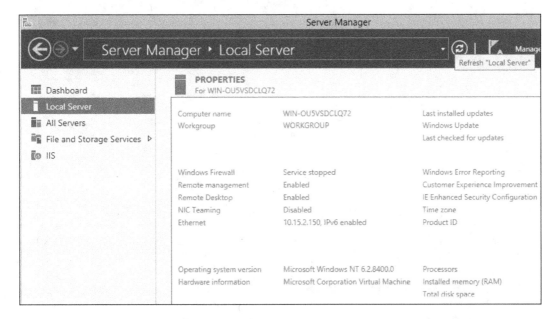

4. When you select the **Computer name** or **Workgroup** options from the **Server Manager** dashboard, it will bring up the old-fashioned **System Properties** window, where you can change the server properties.

5. To configure Windows Server 2012 Server Core, enter the `sconfig` (Server Configuration) command from the command prompt.

6. This will bring up the **Server Configuration** wizard as shown in the following screenshot. From this window, you can change **Name**, **Workgroup**, and so on.

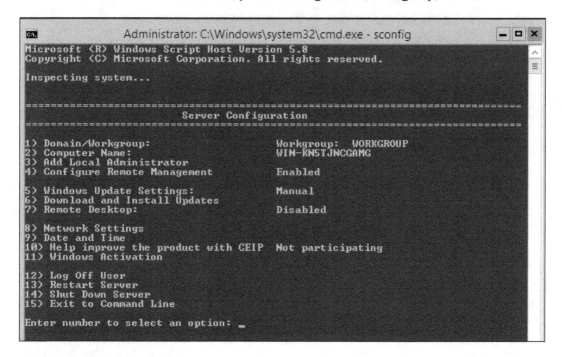

How it works...

The Server Manager in Windows Server 2012 Server with a GUI and sconfig (Server Configuration Wizard) in Windows Server 2012 Server Core, allows you to modify the default server name, IP address, and so on to customize the system based on your requirement.

There's more...

Most of these configurations can also be completed using PowerShell. Since the primary scope of this book is about migrating from Windows Server 2008/R2 to Windows Server 2012, we won't be including the detailed server configuration steps in this book.

I believe now we have a fully functional Windows Server 2012 in the existing Active Directory domain. The next recipe will cover some of the basic administration tasks before we explain the migration procedure in the later recipes of this book.

Installing administration tools (Must know)

In this recipe, we will explain the new features and options available in Windows Server 2012 to manage and administer remote or local servers. This recipe also covers some of the deployment tasks that are relevant for migrating Windows Server 2008/R2 to Windows Server 2012.

Getting ready

Like other operating systems, **Remote Server Administration Tools** (**RSAT**) is available in Windows Server 2012 also. This tool pack includes administration tools, PowerShell cmdlets, and other utilities to manage and administer local and remote servers. This is a feature in Windows Server 2012. It can be added by using the **Add Roles and Features** wizard from **Server Manager**.

In this recipe, I will explain a procedure to deploy Remote Server Administration Tools.

How to do it...

1. Open **Server Manager**.
2. From the **Manage** tab in the top-right section of the screen, select **Add Roles and Features**.

3. Click on **Next** in the **Add Roles and Features Wizard** window.
4. In the **Select Installation Type** window, select **Role-based or Feature-based installation**. Click on **Next**.
5. In the **Select destination server** window, select the **Select a server from the server pool** option and select the server names where you want to deploy the administrative tools. Click on **Next**.

6. Click on **Next** on the **Select server roles** window.

7. In the **Select features** window, select **Remote Server Administration Tools**. It will prompt you to add the required components such as IIS and so on. Click on **Next**.

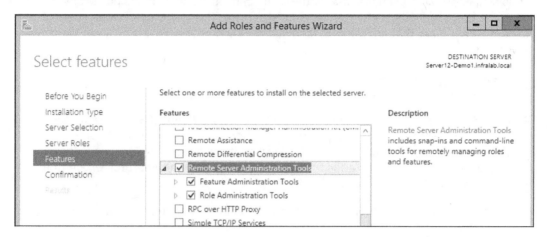

8. In the **Confirm Installation** window, select the **Restart the destination server Automatically if required** option. Click on **Install**.

9. You will see progress in the **Installation Progress** window. The window can be closed but the installation will continue in the background. You can get the status update in the notification section in the **Server Manager** window. You can also export the configuration into an XML file by selecting the **Export Configuration Setting** hyperlink in the bottom of the page.

10. Click on **Close** when the installation finishes.

 The **Remote Server Administration Tools** (**RSAT**) can also be added using PowerShell cmdlet `Add-WindowsFeature`.

How it works...

In the background, Server Manager uses standard **Windows Management Instrumentation** (**WMI**), PowerShell, and the **Distributed Component Object Model** (**DCOM**) to add or remote roles and features to local or remote servers.

There's more...

Most of these administrative tools will be added to the Start screen of the Windows Server 2012. Other tools can be opened by typing the command in the Start screen itself or you will see some of these administrative tools in the **Tools** menu in the **Server Manager** window as shown in the following screenshot:

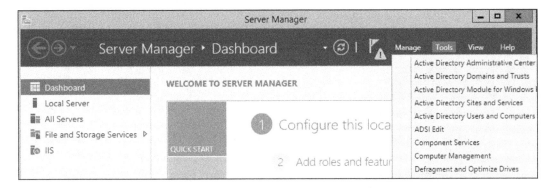

The Remote Server Administration Tools is available for Windows 8 operating systems as a standalone executable application. This can be downloaded from the Microsoft website. It is available for both 32-bit and 64-bit systems.

Remote management is enabled by default on all Windows Server 2012 servers. You can change this configuration from server properties hyperlink.

Working with Server Manager properties (Should know)

In Windows Server 2012, understanding the Server Manager dashboard and its capabilities are essential for an administrator to efficiently manage the servers. The Server Manager starts automatically on a Windows Server 2012 server when the user has local administrator permission. You can change this default behavior by modifying the properties. These details are explained in the following recipe.

If the Server Manager does not open automatically, you can manually open it from the taskbar by clicking on the Server Manager icon as shown in the following screenshot:

By default, the Server Manager polls the information every 10 minutes. However, you can change this configuration from the **Server Manager Properties** window as explained in the following recipe.

How to do it...

1. Open **Server Manager**.

2. From the **Manage** tab on the top–right section of the screen, select **Server Manager Properties**.

3. In the **Server Manager Properties** window, you can change the refresh period in minutes.

4. You will also see an option to disable the Server Manager startup option during the system restart.

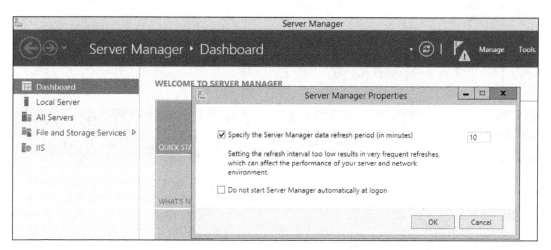

You can manually refresh the status by using the refresh button on the Dashboard.

How it works...

The **Server Manager Properties** window allows you to change the default time interval. The allowed values are from 1 to 14400 minutes. If you want to get a real-time alert, you can decrease the value.

There's more...

You can manage Windows Server 2008 and Windows Server 2008 R2 from the Windows Server 2012 management console. However, the functionality will be limited. The Windows .NET Framework 4 and Management Framework 3 should be installed on the server running the Windows Server 2008 or Windows Server 2008 R2 operating system in order to get the update from these servers onto the new Server Manager.

Adding servers to Server Manager (Should know)

In Windows Server 2012, you have an option to manually add servers to the Server Manager. The following recipe explains this procedure.

How to do it...

1. Open **Server Manager**.

2. From the **Manage** tab on the top-right section of the screen, select **Add Server**.

3. You can add servers from the **Active Directory**, **DNS**, or **Import** tab as shown in the following screenshot:

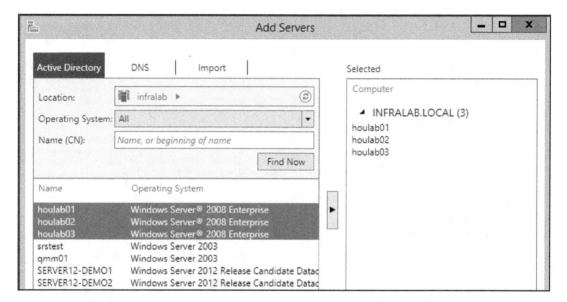

4. Select the appropriate servers using the right arrow button and click on **OK**. You will see these new servers in the Server Manager dashboard.

 At a later stage, unwanted servers can be removed from the list by right-clicking and selecting the **Remove Server** option from the Server Manager dashboard.

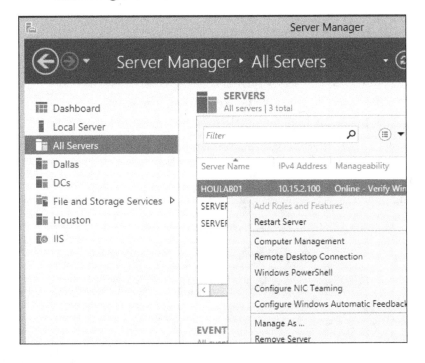

How it works...

The Server Manager uses XML-based configuration files to maintain the list of the servers. These configurations and custom settings are stored in the `%appdata%\Microsoft\Windows\ServerManager\ServerList.xml` and `%appdata%\Microsoft\Windows Client\1.0\user.config` files. These settings can be exported to other servers by copying these files to other servers.

Creating server group (Should know)

With the new server group concept, you can now manage and administer local and remote servers based on roles, features, or custom categories. Server group supports Windows Server 2012, Windows Server 2008/R2, and Windows Server 2003 operating systems (OS). The following recipe explains these procedures.

How to do it...

1. Open **Server Manager**.

2. From the **Manage** tab on the top right, select **Create Server Group**.

3. Enter a name for the group in the **Server Group Name** box.

4. You can add servers from the **Active Directory**, **DNS**, or **Import** tab.

5. Select the appropriate servers using the right-hand side arrow button and click on **OK**. You will see this new group in the Server Manager dashboard.

6. More servers can be added to an existing server group by selecting the **Edit Server Group** option from the Server Manager dashboard.

How it works...

The server group is a logical classification based on the properties of a server. When you add or remove groups, the XML configuration files will get updated to maintain the local list.

Enabling remote desktop (Should know)

The **Remote Desktop Protocol** (**RDP**) is a common method used in server administration. In Windows Server 2012, the new Server Manager is capable of remotely managing multiple servers. However, in certain instances, the administrators have to remotely login to these servers using a remote desktop connection. This procedure is explained in the following recipe:

How to do it...

1. From the Start window, right-click **My Computer** and select **Properties**.
2. This will bring up the old-fashioned **System Properties** page.

3. Select **Remote Settings** from the left-hand side page.
4. From the **Remote** tab, you can modify the remote desktop configuration.

 You can directly open the **System Properties** window from the command prompt by typing the `Systempropertiesremote.exe` command.

Shadowing a remote administration session is not supported in Windows Server 2012.

How it works...

The preceding procedure modifies the remote desktop properties and enables the remote access capabilities on the server.

Add and remove roles and features (Must know)

Additional roles and features can be deployed onto local or remote machines using the same procedure described in the *Installing Administration Tools (Must know)* recipe of this book. In this recipe we will explain a procedure to remove roles and features using Server Manager.

How to do it...

1. Open **Server Manager**.

2. From the **Manage** tab, select the **Remove Roles and Features** option.

3. Click on **Next** on the **Remove Roles and Features Wizard** window.

4. In the **Select Destination Server** window, select the **Select a server from the server pool** option and select the appropriate server name and click on **Next**.

5. Click on **Next** in the **Select server roles** window.

6. Select the appropriate server roles. In this example I am planning to remove graphical tools. So in the **Remote Features** window, uncheck **Graphical Management Tools and Infrastructure** and **Server Graphical Shell**. Uninstalling Graphical Management Tools and Infrastructure will automatically uninstall Server Graphical Shell and Windows PowerShell ISE. Click on **Next**. Server Manager will automatically detect the dependent software and uninstall them if necessary.

7. On the **Confirm Removal** selection, select **Restart the destination Server automatically if required** checkbox and accept the warning message. Click on **Remove**.

How it works...

The preceding procedure adds or removes roles and features from a local or remote server. You can deploy multiple roles and features to multiple servers using this procedure.

There's more...

In the previous 10 recipes, I have explained the Windows Server 2012 installation, configuration, and administration details. With this knowledge, it is now time for you to prepare and migrate your existing environment using Windows Server 2012. In the next few recipes, I will be explaining the details of migrating all services from the current operating system into Windows Server 2012.

Active Directory migration (Must know)

We will start with the Active Directory migration. At this point, we have the proven migration plan and tested all procedures in the lab.

Getting ready

The following prerequisites have to be met before we can introduce the first Windows Server 2012 Domain Controller into the existing Active Directory domain:

- In order to add a Windows Server 2012 Domain Controller, the **Forest Functional Level** (**FFL**) must be Windows Server 2003.
- **ADPREP** is part of the domain controller process and the schema will get upgraded during this process. So the account must have the Schema and Enterprise admins privileges to install the first Windows Server 2012 Domain Controller.
- If there is a firewall between the new server and the existing domain controllers, make sure all the RPC high ports are open between these servers. The domain controller installation and replication can be controlled by a static or a range of RPC ports by modifying the registry on the domain controllers.
- The new Windows 2012 server's primary DNS IP address must be the IP address of an existing domain controller.
- The new server must be able to access the existing Active Directory domain and controllers by **NetBIOS** and **Fully Qualified Domain Name** (**FQDN**).
- If the new domain controller will be in a new site or in a new subnet, make sure to update the Active Directory Sites and Services with this information.

In Windows Server 2012, domain controllers can be remotely deployed by using the Server Manager. The following recipe provides the step-by-step instructions on how to deploy a domain controller in an existing Active Directory environment.

How to do it...

1. Install and configure a Windows Server 2012. Refer to the recipes *Installing Windows Server 2012 (Must know)* and *Configuring Windows Server 2012 (Must know)* for more details.

2. Join the new Windows Server 2012 to the existing Active Directory domain. Refer to the recipe *Configuring Windows Server 2012 (Must know)* for more details.

3. Open **Server Manager**. Navigate to the **All Servers** group in the left-hand side pane.

4. From the **Server Name** box, right-click on the appropriate server and select the **Add Roles and Features** option. You can also select **Add Roles and Features** from the **Manage** menu in the command bar. If the correct server is not listed here, you can manually add it from the **Manage** tab on the top right-hand side and select **Add Server**.

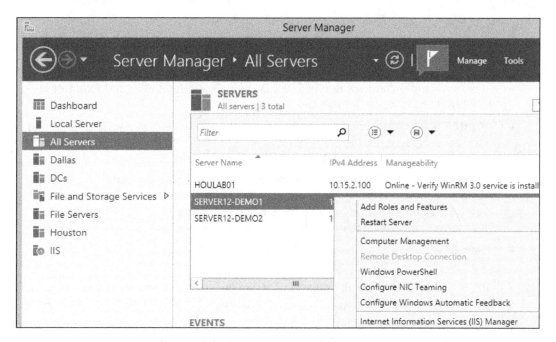

5. Click on **Next** on the **Welcome** window.

6. In the **Select Installation Type** window, select **Role based or Feature based installation**. Click on **Next**.

7. In the **Select destination server** window, select **Select a server from the server pool** option and the correct server from the **Server Pool** box. Click on **Next**.

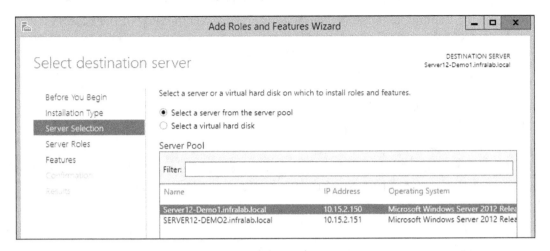

8. On the **Select server roles** window, select **Active Directory Domain Services**. You will see a pop-up window to confirm the installation of **Group Policy Management Tool**. It is not required to install the administrative tools on a domain controller. However, this tool is required for the Group Policy Object management and administration. Click on **Next**.

9. Click on **Next** in the **Select features** window.

10. Click on **Next** on the **Active Directory Domain Services** window.

11. In the **Confirm Installation Selections** window, select the **Restart the destination server automatically if required** option. In the pop-up window click on **Yes** to confirm the restart option and click on **Install**. This will begin the installation process.

12. You will see the progress on the installation window itself. This window can be closed without interrupting the installation process. You can get the status update from the notification section in the command bar as shown in the following screenshot:

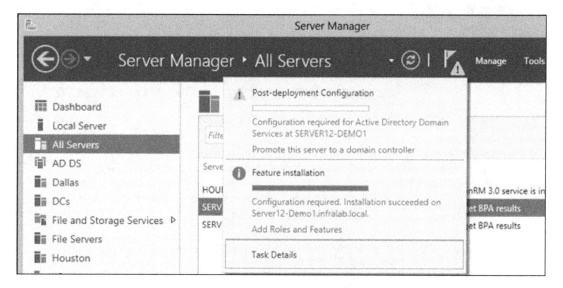

13. The **Post-deployment Configuration** option needs to be completed after the Active Directory Domain Services role installation. This process will promote the new server as a domain controller.

14. From the notification window, select **Promote this server to a domain controller** hyperlink.

15. From the **Deployment Configuration** window, you should be able to:

   ❑ Install a new forest

   ❑ Install a new child domain

   ❑ Add an additional domain controller for an existing domain

   ❑ Specify alternative credentials for the domain controller promotion, and so on

16. Since our goal is to install an additional domain controller to an existing domain, select the **Add a domain controller to an existing domain** option. Click on **Next**.

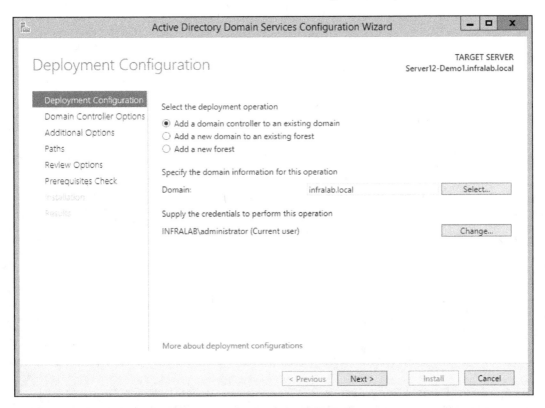

17. In the **Domain Controller Options** window, you will see the following options:

   ❑ **Domain Name System (DNS) server**

   ❑ **Global Catalog (GC)**

   ❑ **Read only Domain controller (RODC)**

   ❑ **Site name:**

   ❑ **Type the Directory Service Restore Mode (DSRM) password**

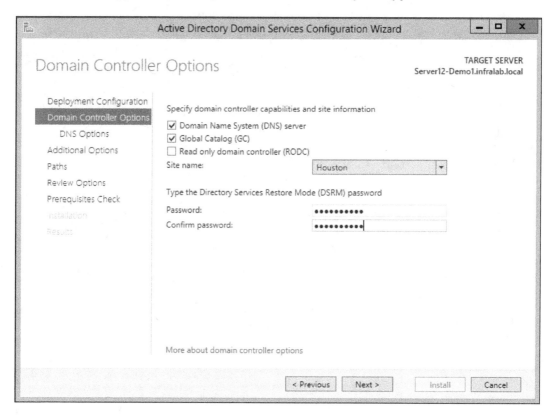

18. Select **Domain Name System (DNS) server** and **Global Catalog (GC)** checkboxes and provide the **Directory Services Restore Mode** (**DSRM**) password. Click on **Next**.

19. Click on **Next** on the **DNS Options** window.

20. In the **Additional Options** window you will see the following options:

   ❑ **Install from media**

   ❑ **Replicate from**

21. Accept the default options unless you have technical reasons to modify these. Click on **Next**.

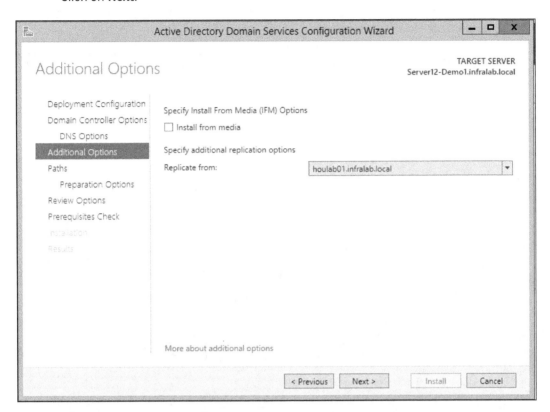

22. In the **Paths** window, you can specify the AD Database, Log, and SYSVOL locations. Select the appropriate locations and then click on **Next**.

Review the Microsoft **Infrastructure Planning and Design (IPD)** guides for best practices recommendations. For performance improvements, it is recommended to place database, log, and so on in separate drives.

23. Click on **Next** on the **Preparation Options** window. During this process the Active Directory Schema and Domain Preparation will happen in the background.

24. You should be able to review the selected option on the next screen. You can export these settings and configurations to a PowerShell script by clicking on the **View Script** option in the bottom-right corner of the screen. This script can be used for future domain controller deployments.

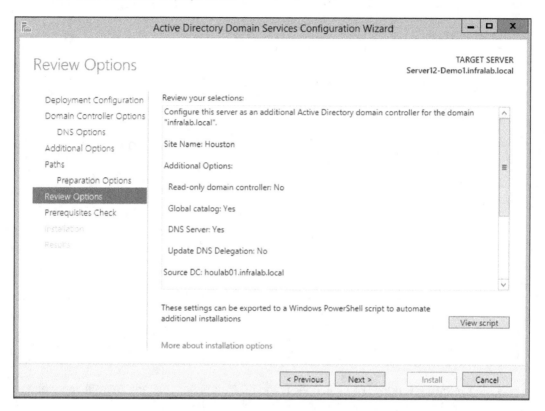

25. Click on **Next** to continue with the installation.

26. The prerequisite checking process will happen in the background. You will see the result in the **Prerequisites Check** window. This is a new enhancement in Windows Server 2012. Review the result and click on **Install**.

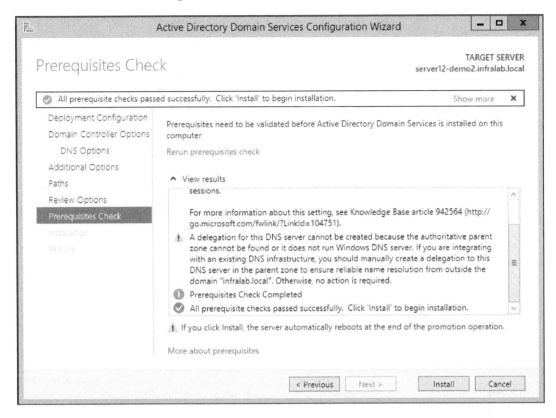

27. The progress of the domain controller promotion will display on the **Installation** window.

28. The following warning message will be displayed on the destination server before it restarts the server:

 You can review the `%systemroot%\debug\dcpromo.log` and `%SystemRoot%\debug\netsetup.log` log files to get more information about DCPROMO and domain join-related issues.

How it works...

The preceding process adds an additional domain controller in the exiting Active Directory forest. At this time the current Active Directory environment has both Windows Server 2008/R2 and Windows Server 2012 domain controllers. This is technically called a **mixed mode environment**. The Server Manager will be updated with the new roles and features on this server as shown in the following screenshot:

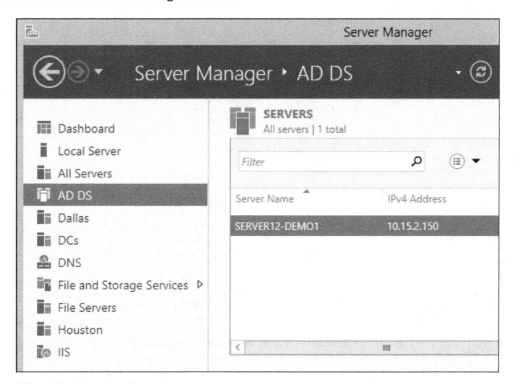

There's more...

If you are planning to perform an in-place upgrade of a domain controller (the first Windows Server 2012 Domain Controller), the **Active Directory Schema and Domain Preparation** (**ADPREP**) commands need to be run manually. The `ADPrep.exe` tool is available in the `D:\Support\Adprep\` folder in the Windows Server 2012 installation media. Keep in mind that the ADPREP tool is only available in a 64-bit version. After the schema upgrade, the schema version can be manually verified by using the following `dsquery` command:

```
dsquery * cn=schema,cn=configuration,dc=domain,dc=com -scope base -attr
objectVersion
```

```
Administrator: Command Prompt                    _  □  x

C:\>dsquery * cn=schema,cn=configuration,dc=infralab,dc=local -scope base -attr objectVersion
  objectVersion
  56
```

The `objectVersion` value is 56 for the Windows Server 2012 schema.

> You can also identify `objectVersion` based on the LDIF filename.
> The latest `Sch56.ldf` filename indicates that schema version as 56.
> Their files are available in the `D:\Support\Adprep\` folder.

The Group Policy Preparation (`/gprep`) is not a requirement while adding Windows Server 2012 Domain Controllers to the existing domain. However, in order to use the **Result Set of Policy** (**RSoP**) in planning mode, the `/gprep` process needs to be completed by using the `adprep/gpprep` command. The **Read Only Domain Controller Preparation** (`adprep / rodocprep`) process needs to be completed before you can add the **Read Only Domain Controllers** (**RODC**).

> You can review the ADPREP log file (`%windir%\System32\Debug\` `Adprep\Logs`) to get more information about ADPREP-related issues.

The health of the domain controller and domain can be verified by using native tools such as DCDiag. Microsoft has a new tool called **ADRELSTATUS (Active Directory Replication Status Tool)** to verify and monitor Active Directory replication. As a best practice it is recommended to have multiple domain controllers for the same domain. You can use the same procedure to add more domain controllers. It is also recommended to install Remote Server Administration Tools on a Windows 8 machine to administer Active Directory instead of directly logging on to a domain controller.

FSMO role transfer/migration (Must know)

Transferring or migrating a **Flexible Single Master Operations** (**FSMO**) role is not a requirement at this point. However, some of the new features in Windows Server 2012 such as cloning of virtual domain controllers, and so on, won't be available until the **PDC emulator** (**PDCe**) role is transferred to a Windows Server 2012 Domain Controller. To take advantage of improvements in RID Master, this role must be running on Windows Server 2012 Domain Controller. The placement and optimization of FMSO roles is beyond the scope of this book. For this scenario, we will be moving all FMSO roles (Schema, Domain Naming Master, PDCe, Infrastructure Master, and RID) to a new Windows Server 2012 Domain Controller.

How to do it...

Using **PowerShell**:

1. Log on to Windows Server 2012 and open the PowerShell window.

2. In the PowerShell window enter the following cmdlet:

   ```
   Move-ADDirectoryServerOperationMasterRole -Identity "DCName☒
   -OperationMasterRole SchemaMaster,DomainNamingMaster,PDCEmulator,
   RIDMaster,InfrastructureMaster
   ```

3. To confirm the FSMO transfer, press *Y*.

```
PS C:\> Move-ADDirectoryServerOperationMasterRole -Identity Server12-Demo1 -OperationMasterRole SchemaMaster,DomainNamir
gMaster,PDCEmulator,RIDMaster,InfrastructureMaster

Move Operation Master Role
Do you want to move role 'SchemaMaster' to server 'Server12-Demo1.infralab.local' ?
[Y] Yes  [A] Yes to All  [N] No  [L] No to All  [S] Suspend  [?] Help (default is "Y"): y

Move Operation Master Role
Do you want to move role 'DomainNamingMaster' to server 'Server12-Demo1.infralab.local' ?
[Y] Yes  [A] Yes to All  [N] No  [L] No to All  [S] Suspend  [?] Help (default is "Y"): y

Move Operation Master Role
Do you want to move role 'PDCEmulator' to server 'Server12-Demo1.infralab.local' ?
[Y] Yes  [A] Yes to All  [N] No  [L] No to All  [S] Suspend  [?] Help (default is "Y"): y

Move Operation Master Role
Do you want to move role 'RIDMaster' to server 'Server12-Demo1.infralab.local' ?
[Y] Yes  [A] Yes to All  [N] No  [L] No to All  [S] Suspend  [?] Help (default is "Y"): y

Move Operation Master Role
Do you want to move role 'InfrastructureMaster' to server 'Server12-Demo1.infralab.local' ?
[Y] Yes  [A] Yes to All  [N] No  [L] No to All  [S] Suspend  [?] Help (default is "Y"): y
PS C:\> _
```

Using **MMC**:

1. Log on to the Windows Server 2012 Server or Windows 8 machine and open the **Active Directory User and Computers (ADUC)** MMC.

2. Right-click on the domain name and select **Operations Masters...**.

3. In the **Operations Masters** tab, click on the **Change** button to transfer the FMSO role to the new Windows Server 2012 Domain Controller. Repeat these steps for transferring the PDC emulator and Infrastructure Master roles.

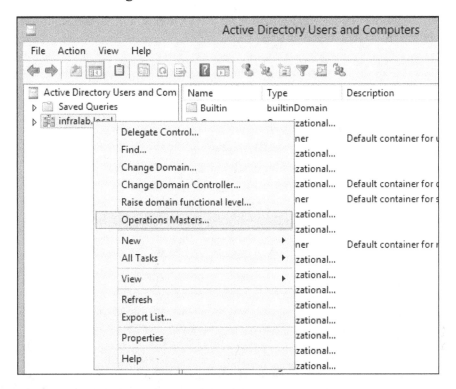

The forest-specific role—**Domain Naming Master**—can be transferred using Active Directory Domains and Trust MMC.

1. Log on to the Windows Server 2012 or Windows 8 machine and open the **Active Directory Domains and Trust** console.

2. Right-click on the **Active Directory Domains and Trust** node and select **Operations Master...**.

3. In the **Operations Master** tab click on the **Change** button to transfer the Domain Naming Master FMSO role.

The forest-specific role—**Schema Master FMSO**—can be transferred using the Active Directory Schema MMC. You may need to register schmmgmt.dll using the regsvr32 schmmgmt.dll command in order to view the Active Directory Schema MMC.

1. Log on to the Windows Server 2012 or Windows 8 machine and open the **Active Directory Schema** console.

2. Right-click on the **Active Directory Schema** node and select **Operations Master...**.

3. In the **Operations Masters** tab, click on the **Change** button to transfer the Schema Master FMSO role.

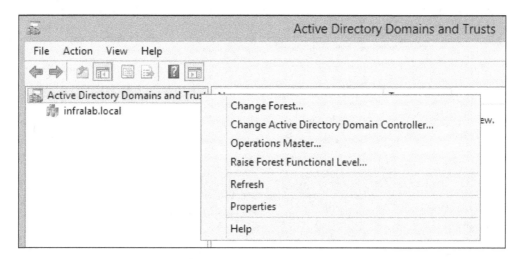

How it works...

The Move-ADDirectoryServerOperationMasterRole PowerShell cmdlet is part of the Active Directory PowerShell module. Instead of using FSMO roles, you could use numeric values. For example, 0 for PDC emulator, 1 for RID Master, 2 for Infrastructure Master, 3 for Schema Master, and 4 for Domain Naming Maser.

There's more...

Alternatively, the NTDSUTIL tool can be used to transfer the FSMO roles. The domain-specific roles—RID, PDC, and Infrastructure Master—can be transferred using the **Active Directory User and Computer** (**ADUC**) tool.

The FSMO roles can be verified using the Netdom Query FSMO command as shown in the following screenshot:

```
C:\>Netdom Query FSMO
Schema master                houlab01.infralab.local
Domain naming master         houlab01.infralab.local
PDC                          houlab01.infralab.local
RID pool manager             houlab01.infralab.local
Infrastructure master        houlab01.infralab.local
The command completed successfully.
```

The following PowerShell cmdlet can also be used to verify the FMSO roles:

```
Get-ADDomain domain.com | Format-List PDCEmulator,RIDMaster,Infrastructur
eMaster
```

```
Get-ADForest domain.com | Format-List SchemaMaster,DomainNamingMaster
```

 The Get-ADDomain PowerShell cmdlet is part of Active Directory PowerShell module.

Windows Server Migration Tools (Must know)

Some of the migrations can be accomplished by using native and built-in tools. So far we were using the built-in tools to migrate these services. Microsoft has included the latest version of the Windows Server Migration Tools in Windows Server 2012. We will be using this tool in the rest of the migrations. These are PowerShell cmdlets and are part of the Windows Server Migration Tools PowerShell module. In Windows Server 2008 and Windows Server 2008 R2, the source and target server have to be in the same subnet to migrate data using this tool. However, the new version of the Server Migration tool supports cross-subnet migrations. The TCP and UDP ports 7000, 7001, and 7002 must be open between source and target servers to support this scenario.

Getting ready

The following key PowerShell cmdlets will be used for this migration effort:

- Export-SmigServerSetting: Export role, feature, and so on from the source server to a target server
- Import-SmigServerSetting: Import role, feature, and so on from an export file
- Send-SmigServerData: Send/migrate data and its associated permissions, properties, and so on from the source server
- Receive-SmigServerData: Receive/copy data and its associated permissions, properties, and so on to the target server

It is time to install Windows Server Migration Tools on the Windows Server 2012. It is a best practice to use the latest version of the tool even if the older versions are available on the source servers.

How to do it...

1. Log on to a Windows Server 2012.

2. Open **Server Manager**. From **Server Manager**, install the **Windows Server Migration Tools** feature. Refer to the *Add and remove roles and features (Must know)* recipe for role and feature installation details.

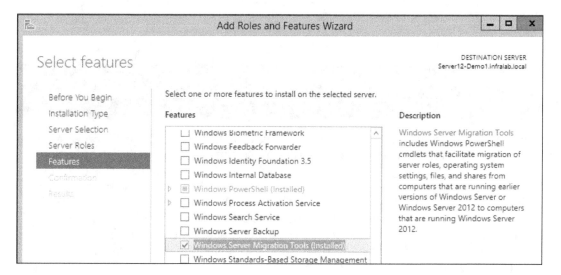

3. From the Start screen, right-click on **Command Prompt** and select the **Run as administrator** option.

4. Change the directory to C:\Windows\System32\ServerMigraitonTool. Run the SmigDeploy.exe /Package /Architecture amd64 /os WS08 /Path /C:\MigTools\ command. This will create a migration tool package for 64-bit servers in the C:\MigTools folder.

You can change the `/architecture` value to create an application package for 32-bit servers.

```
C:\Windows\System32\ServerMigrationTools>SmigDeploy.exe /package /architecture a
md64 /os WS08 /path C:\MigTools\
SmigDeploy.exe is checking for prerequisites.
─────────────────────────────────────────────────────────────────────────────
SmigDeploy.exe is copying Windows Server Migration Tools files to C:\MigTools\SM
T_ws08_amd64.
─────────────────────────────────────────────────────────────────────────────
```

 The SmigDeploy.exe tool creates a migration tool installation package. This package can be directly copied over to the source Windows Server 2008 and Windows Server 2008 R2 servers. Copy the `C:\MigTools` folder to a network share. We will be using this migration package for the rest of the migrations.

How it works...

Copy the `C:\MigTools` folder to a network share. For this scenario, I will be copying the `C:\MigTools` folder to the `\\HOU-MGR-01` server and this will be referenced in the migrations described in this book.

There's more...

At this point the Windows Server Migration Tools for a 64-bit server is available on a network share. This package can be copied to the source and target servers for the migration. No other configuration is required. The necessary parameters will be configured based on the role or feature that we will migrate.

If you have a 32-bit server, you can generate a 32-bit installation package by modifying the `/Architecture` parameter in the preceding command.

Dynamic Host Configuration Protocol (DHCP) migration (Must know)

In this recipe I will explain a procedure for migrating DHCP scope and lease information using the Windows Server Migration Tools. Migrating infrastructure services such as DHCP, DNS, WINS, and so on will have some impact on network operations. So make sure to schedule a maintenance window and place proper change control before you perform these activities.

If the DHCP role is not installed on the target server, the Windows Server Migration Tools will install it during the migration process. However, in this scenario, we will be manually installing the DHCP role and authorizing the DHCP server in Active Directory.

The following diagram explains the high level steps involved in this migration:

How to do it...

1. Log on to Windows Server 2012.

2. Open **Server Manager**. From the **Server Manager** option, install the **DHCP Server** role. Refer to the *Add and remove roles and features (Must know)* recipe for roles and feature installation details.

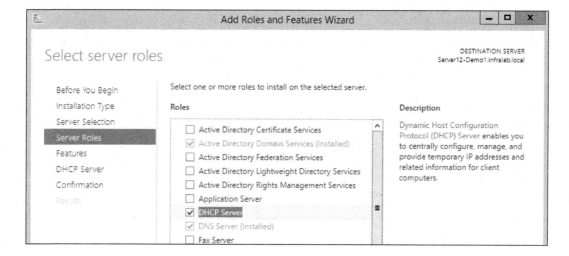

3. From the **DHCP Admin** console, authorize the new DHCP server in Active Directory.

4. Log on to the source DHCP server. Copy the migration tool package from `\\HOU-MGR-01\MigTools` to `C:\MigTools`.

5. Stop the **DHCP Server** service.

6. Open **Command Prompt** with elevated permission and navigate to the `C:\MigTools` folder. Run the `SmigDeploy.exe` command. This will register the migration tool on the source server and open a PowerShell window as shown in the following screenshot:

The PowerShell and .NET Framework are prerequisites for this tool.

After you register the `SmigDeploy.exe` tool, Windows Server Migration Tools will be added to the **Administration Tools** menu on the local server. You can uninstall this tool by running the `SmigDeploy.exe / Unregister` command.

7. The next step is to export the current DHCP configuration from the source server. From the PowerShell window type `Export-SmigServerSetting -FeatureID DHCP -Path C:\DHCPExport\` cmdlet. It will prompt you for a password for the export file. Hit *Enter* to continue with the export process. The export file will be in the `C:\DHCPExport` folder.

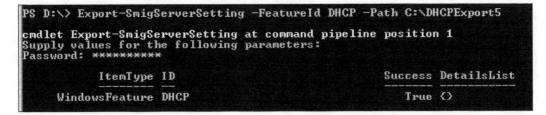

8. Copy this export file (`C:\DHCPExport\svrmig.mig`) over to the target Windows Server 2012 DHCP server.

9. The next step is to import this file onto the new DHCP server. Log on to the target Windows Server 2012 server and open **Windows Server Migration Tools** from the Start window as an administrator. If this role is not locally installed on the server, you can copy the installation package from the `\\HOU-MGR-01\MigTools` folder and run the `SmigDeploy.exe` tool.

10. From the PowerShell window, run the `Import-SmigServerSetting -FeatureID DHCP -Path D:\DHCPExport` cmdlet and hit *Enter*. You need to provide only the folder name.

   As I mentioned before, if the DHCP feature was not installed, the migration tool will install this feature as shown in the following screenshot:

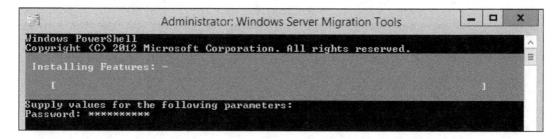

11. Since we already installed the DHCP feature, it will start the import process. You need to provide the same password as configured in the export process.

```
PS C:\Windows\system32> cd\
PS C:\> Import-SmigServerSetting -FeatureId DHCP -Path C:\folder2

cmdlet Import-SmigServerSetting at command pipeline position 1
Supply values for the following parameters:
Password: **********

              ItemType ID                                Success DetailsList
              _____ __                                _____ _____
...tureInstallation DHCP                                 True {}
       WindowsFeature DHCP                                True {}
WARNING: A restart of the local computer is required for changes to complete.
```

12. The new server needs to be restarted after the import process has completed.

How it works...

The preceding process migrates DHCP information onto the new Windows Server 2012 server. At this point the new DHCP server will have all the DHCP scope and lease information.

There's more...

You can verify the scope and lease information from the DHCP admin console. The IP helper address on the router has to be changed with the new DHCP server's IP address if it is configured with the old DHCP server's IP address. Once you verified these configurations, the old DHCP server can be decommissioned. Windows Server 2012 provides high-availability and failover capability for DHCP. You may want to take advantage of this new feature right away.

The DHCP scope and lease information can also be migrated using Netsh Export and Netsh Import commands.

DNS migration (Should know)

If the DNS zone is **Active Directory Integrated** (**ADI**), the zone information will be replicated as part of the Active Directory replication. The scope of the replication is based on the Replication configuration in the zone itself as shown in the following screenshot:

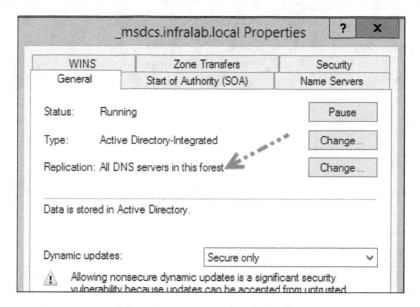

If the zone is Active Directory Integrated and the proper replication scope is configured, you don't need to perform any other migration for the DNS zone. Both forward lookup and reverse lookup zones will replicate to the new Windows Server 2012 Domain Controller during the Active Directory replication.

However, if you have a primary or secondary zone on a standalone server or a member server, you need to perform a migration. There are many ways to achieve this. One option is to perform the migration using a secondary to primary conversion method. Then decommission the old DNS server. Before the DNS zone can be replicated, you need to make sure that the zone transfer is allowed to the new Windows Server 2012 server. These settings can be changed from the **Zone Transfers** tab as shown in the following screenshot:

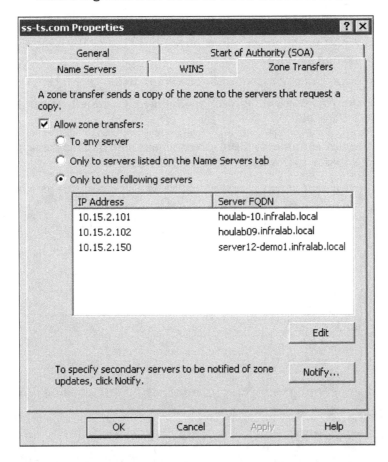

To migrate a DNS zone using the secondary to primary method, refer to the following recipe.

How to do it...

1. Create a secondary zone on the new Windows Server 2012 server.

    i.   Open the **DNS Management** console.

    ii. Right-click on the **Forward Lookup Zone** node. Click on **New Zone**.

    iii. Click on **Next** on the **Welcome** window.

    iv. Select **Secondary Zone** as the **Zone Type**. Click on **Next**.

    v.   Enter the zone name. Click on **Next**.

    vi. On the **Master DNS Servers** window, enter the IP address of the primary DNS server.

    vii. Click on **Finish**.

2. Convert the secondary zone to primary zone.

    i. Verify that the zone information has been completely transferred over to the new server.

    ii. Right-click on the zone and go to **Properties**.

    iii. From the **General** Tab, click on **Change**. Select the zone type as **Primary**. Click on **OK**.

3. Verify the **Start of Authority (SOA)** tab and make sure that the primary server is updated with your new Windows Server 2012 name.

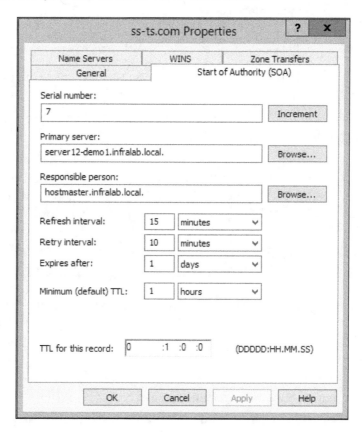

4. Verify the **Name Servers** tab for name servers.

5. Repeat the same procedure for other DNS zones and decommission the old DNS server.

How it works...

The preceding method creates a secondary DNS zone on Windows Server 2012 and converts them to a primary DNS zone after the zone replication. After the DNS zone conversion, Windows Server 2008/R2 and Windows Server 2012 servers will have the Primary DNS zone.

There's more...

The other option is to use the `dnscmd` command. The following commands can be used to export and import zone information between two DNS servers:

```
Export - dnscmd /zoneexport <ZoneName> <ExportFileName>
Import - dnscmd /zoneadd /Primary /File < ExportFileName>
```

The `dnscmd` command is still available on Windows Server 2012. However, this command may be discontinued in the future versions of the product or release. So it is recommended to use the PowerShell cmdlet for the future use. The DnsServer PowerShell module has many cmdlets which can support DNS migration scenarios.

Unless you have valid business and technical requirements, it is a best practice to use the Active Directory Integrated zone. Also, you may want to look at the **DNS Security Extensions** (**DNSSEC**) in Windows Server 2012 and how it can be beneficial to your environment.

Data and file server migration (Must know)

File server or data migration can be achieved by migrating the data from the existing server using tools such as Microsoft Robocopy and Microsoft File Server Migration Tool (FSMT), or directly presenting the storage Logical Unit Number (LUNs) onto a new server. In this scenario, I will be explaining the data migration procedure using Windows Server Migration Tools. `Send-SmigServerData` and `Receive-SmigServerData` are the two PowerShell cmdlets that we will use for this migration.

The `Send-SmigServerData` cmdlet, as it sounds, is responsible for sending (migrating) data from the source server. This tool can migrate folders, files, permission, share, and so on. However, it doesn't support migrating any **Encrypted File Systems** (**EFS**). Unlike other cmdlets in the Windows Server Migration Tools, the `Send-SmigServerData` cmdlet does not store the data in a staging area or an export file. It will directly copy over to the target server. So the required ports (7000, 7001, and 7002) must be open between the source and target servers. The `Receive-SmigServerData` cmdlet has to be running on the target server to be able to receive the migrated data. The `Send-SmigServerData` and `Receive-SmigServerData` cmdlets have to be running on the source and target servers at the same time. The default time out value is five minutes, but this value can be changed by modifying the registry.

For this migration, we need to run the `Send-SmigServerData` cmdlet on the source server and `Receive-SmigServerData` cmdlet on the target server. The following diagram graphically represents the high-level tasks:

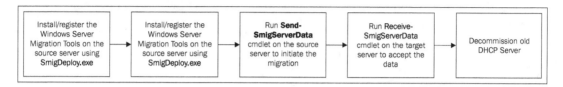

The following recipe explains the data migration procedure.

How to do it...

1. Log on to the source file server and copy the previously created Windows Server Migration Tools package from the `\\HOU-MGR-01\MigTools` folder to `C:\MigTools` folder on the local server.

2. Open **Command Prompt** with elevated privilege and navigate to `C:\MigTools`.

3. From the `C:\MigTools` folder, give the `SmigDeploy.exe` command. This will register the Windows Server Migration Tools on the server and open a PowerShell window as shown in the following screenshot:

4. If you close the PowerShell window by mistake, you can re-open it from the **Windows Server Migration Tools** menu in **Administrative Tools**.

5. At this time you need to make sure that the users are not connected to the file server or are not accessing the data from this server. If you have any backup or any other software running on this server, make sure to disable them during the migration process.

6. Run the following cmdlet from the PowerShell window to initiate the migration process:

```
Send-SmigServerData -ComputerName server12-demo1 -SourcePath ⊠D:\
Hou-Fil-Data-01⊠ -DestinationPath ⊠C:\Data\⊠ -Recurse -Include All
-Force
```

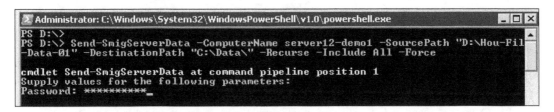

In the preceding command, `-ComputerName` is the target file server, `-SourcePath` is the location of the source data, and you also need to specify the destination location on the target server by using the `-DestinationPath` parameter. You have the following three options that can be used with the `-Include` parameter:

- `All`: This migrates data and share
- `Data`: This copies only the files and folders and their associated permission
- `Share`: This copies only the share properties and permission

The `-Force` parameter overwrites the existing files on the target server if the source files are current.

It will prompt you for a password. Once it accepts the password you will have five minutes to run the `Receive-SmigServerData` cmdlet on the target server. As you can see in the following screenshot, the source server is waiting for the destination server request to transfer the data.

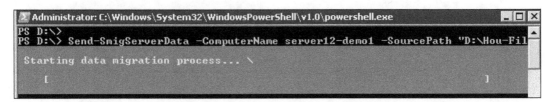

7. Log on to the target Windows Server 2012 file server. Copy the Windows Server Migration Tools package from `\\HOU-MGR-01\Migtools` to the `C:\MigTools` folder.

8. Open **Command Prompt** with elevated privilege and navigate to C:\MigTools.

9. From the C:\MigTools folder, type the SmigDeploy.exe command. This will register the Windows Server Migration Tools on the source server and open a PowerShell window.

10. From the PowerShell command window, type the Receive-SmigServerData cmdlet. It will prompt you for the same password which you used on the source server.

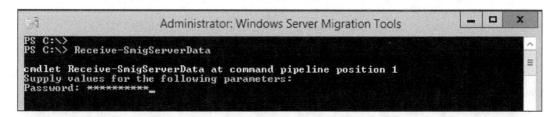

11. Once the password is validated, it will copy the data from the source server.

12. A migration summary report will be generated as shown in the following screenshot:

```
Administrator: C:\Windows\System32\WindowsPowerShell\v1.0
WarningMessageList   : {}

ItemType             : Folder
SourceLocation       : D:\Hou-Fil-Data-01\1
DestinationLocation  : C:\Data\1
Success              : True
Size                 : 0
ErrorDetails         :
Error                : None
WarningMessageList   : {}

ItemType             : Folder
SourceLocation       : D:\Hou-Fil-Data-01\2
DestinationLocation  : C:\Data\2
Success              : True
Size                 : 0
ErrorDetails         :
Error                : None
WarningMessageList   : {}

ItemType             : Share
SourceLocation       : d:\hou-fil-data-01\1 [1]
DestinationLocation  : C:\Data\\1 [1]
Success              : True
Size                 : 0
ErrorDetails         :
Error                : None
WarningMessageList   : {}
```

How it works...

Once you have validated the data between the source and target servers you can decommission the old file server. If drive mapping or shares are enabled through Group Policy Object or Group Policy Preference, the policies will have to be updated with the new server name.

Printer and print server migration (Must know)

For migrating printers from a Windows Server 2008 or Windows Server 2008 R2 server to Windows Server 2012, we will be using the Print Management console. This administration tool is part of the Print and Document Services role in Windows Server 2012. This tool can be used to migrate printers from both x86 and x64 servers. If you are migrating printers from a 32-bit server, make sure to install 64-bit drivers prior to the migration. The print drivers, queues, shares, directory listing, and security settings can be migrated using this migration tool. During the migration you will have an option to list (publish) these printers in Active Directory. So if these printers were listed in Active Directory previously, the migration utility can maintain the same configuration after the migration.

The following diagram graphically represents all the high-level tasks:

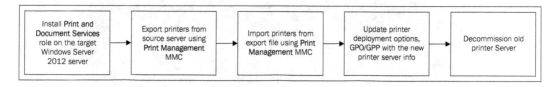

How to do it...

The following steps will help you migrate printers using the print management console:

1. Log on to the new Windows Server 2012 server.

2. Open **Server Manager** and install the **Print and Document Services** role. Refer to the *Add and remove roles and features (Must know)* recipe for role and feature installation details.

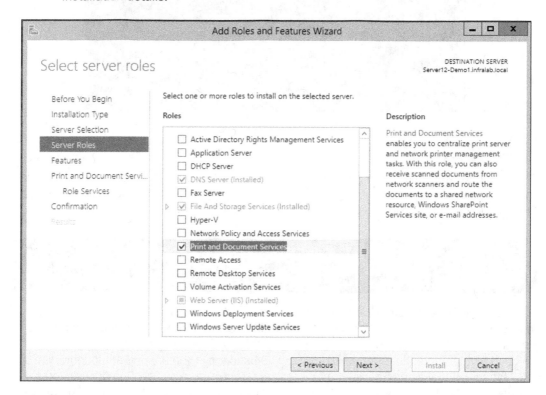

3. On the **Select role services** window, select the **Print Server** service. Click on **Next** and complete the role installation.

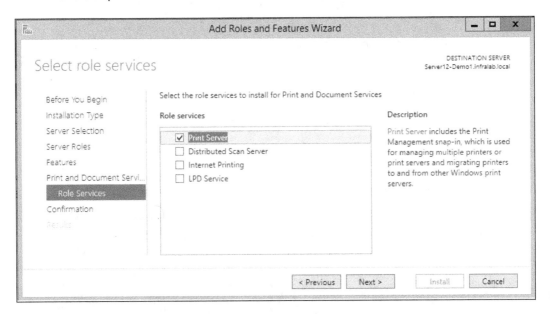

4. Open the **Print Management** console from the Start screen.

5. Right-click on the **Print Management** node and select the **Migrate Printers...** option.

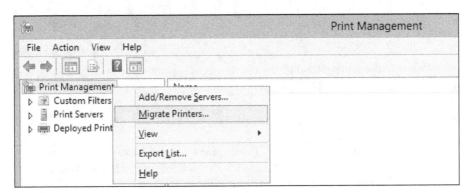

6. Select **Export printer queues and printer drivers to a file** option and click on **Next**.

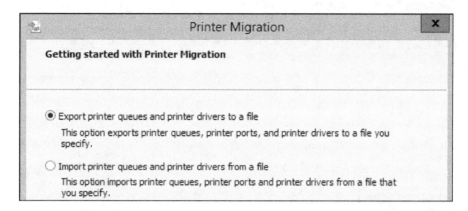

7. On the **Select a print server** window, select the source print server in the **Server name** box. Make sure that the account you are using can access the source server from the target server and has full permission on both servers. Click on **Next**.

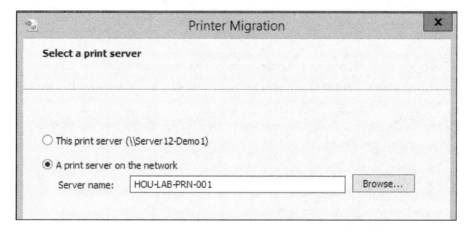

8. The discovery process will identify **Print Queues**, **Print Drivers**, and **Printer Processors**. You will see this information in the **Review the list of items to be exported** window. Review the items and click on **Next** to continue.

9. In the **Select file location** window, select a destination folder. Click on **Next**. You will see the progress in the next window. You can also open **Printer Migration Events** in **Event Viewer** to get more details as shown in the following screenshot:

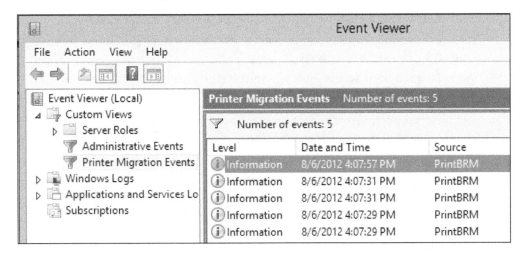

10. Click on **Finish** to complete the export process.

11. The next step is to import these printers onto the new Windows Server 2012 print server. Right-click on the **Print Management** node and select the **Migrate Printers...** option.

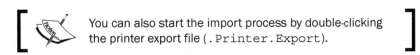

> You can also start the import process by double-clicking the printer export file (`.Printer.Export`).

12. This time, select **Import printer queues and printer drivers from a file**. Click on **Next**.

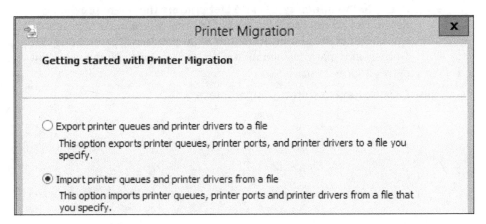

13. In the **Select the file location** window, select the export file. Click on **Next**.

14. The printer information can be reviewed in the **Review the list of items to be imported** window. Click on **Next**.

15. In the **Select a print server** window, select the destination Windows Server 2012 print server. Click on **Next**.

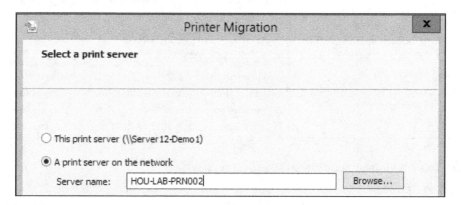

16. In the **Select import options** window, you have the fields **Import mode** and List in the **directory**:

   i.   In **Import mode** we have **Keep existing printers** and **Overwrite existing printers**. Since we are migrating into a new print server, our assumption is that we don't have any printers available on this new server. So we will select the **Overwrite existing printers** option.

   ii.   In **List in the directory** we have **List printers that were previously listed**, **List all printers**, and **Do not list any printers**. For this scenario, we will select the **List printers that were previously listed** option. This will automatically update the Active Directory with the new print server information.

   iii.   Click on **Next** to start the import process.

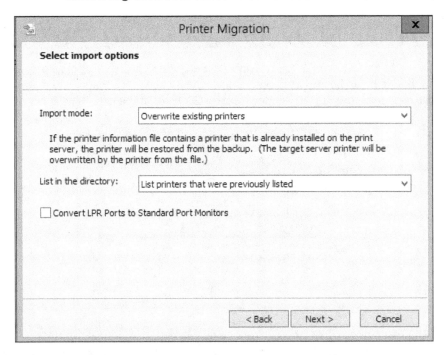

17. Click on **Finish** to complete the process.

How it works...

At this point all the printers are migrated onto the new printer server. The migration log and Event Viewer will provide more information about the migration process and result. If you don't see any errors in any of these logs, you can start decommissioning the old print servers. If the printer mappings or automatic deployment of printer are configured through Group Policy Object or Group Policy Preference, these policies should to be updated with the new printer server information.

There's more...

Instead of using the Print Management console, you could use the `Printbrm.exe` command line tools to achieve the same result. By default, these tools are located in the `C:\Windows\ System32\spool\tools` folder. The `Printbrm.exe -s <\\SourceServer> -b -f <File>` command will export the printers from the source server and the `Printbrm.exe -s <\\TargetServer> -r -f <File>` command will import printers into the target server.

Hyper-V migration (Should know)

As you know, in Windows Server 2008 or Windows Server 2008 R2, an export file was a requirement before it can be imported onto a new Hyper-V server. I am sure you are all familiar with the following error message in Windows Server 2008/R2 if the export file is not available:

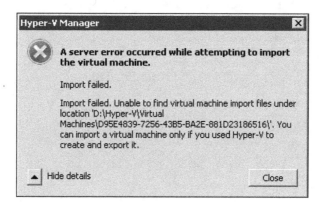

In Windows Server 2012, Microsoft supports importing virtual machines (VM) into a Hyper-V host without an export (.exp) file. In other words, you can use raw Hyper-V files from the source server. The import and export feature is also available.

Installation and configuration of Windows Server 2012 Hyper-V is beyond the scope of this book. So for this migration scenario, the assumption is that the target Windows Server 2012 Hyper-V servers are in place and running. Before you begin the export and import process, you need to make sure that the local or network share has enough storage space to accommodate these virtual machines. Another common issue related to virtual machine migration is the permission issues. The export/import folder must have full permission for the user and computer account.

The following diagram provides high level task details:

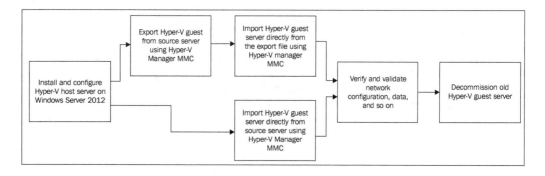

We will start the migration process without an export file.

How to do it...

1. Shutdown the source Hyper-V guest machine.

2. Log on to the target Windows Server 2012 Hyper-V server and open **Hyper-V Manager** from the Start screen.

3. Right-click on the Hyper-V host server node and click on the **Import Virtual Machine** option.

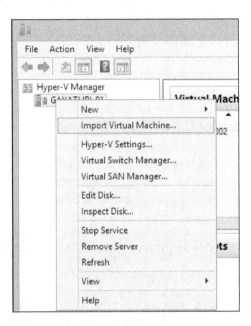

4. In the **Before You Begin** window click on **Next**.

5. In the **Locate Folder** window, specify the location of the existing virtual machine from the source server. Click on **Next**.

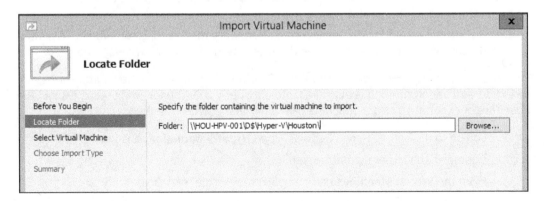

6. On the **Select Virtual Machine** window, select the correct server name. Click on **Next**.

7. You will see the following options on the **Choose Import Type** window:

    i.   **Register the virtual machine in-place (use the existing unique ID)**

    ii. **Restore the virtual machine (use the existing unique ID)**

    iii. **Copy the virtual machine (create a new unique ID)**

8. Click on **Next**.

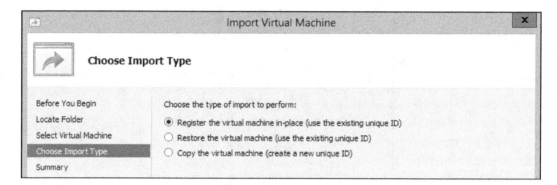

9. In the **Choose Folders for Virtual Machine files** window, you can change the default location of the **Configuration**, **Snapshot store**, and **Smart Paging** folders. Click on **Next**.

> The **Smart Paging** is part of the dynamic memory feature in Hyper-V 3.0. It provides an efficient memory management option during the server restart process if the minimum memory is less than the startup memory.

10. In the **Choose Folders to Store Virtual Hard Disks** window, select the location of the hard disks. Click on **Next**.

11. Review the configuration details on the **Summary** window. Click on **Finish**. The import process will start and you will see the progress in the Hyper-V manager console.

For some reason, you cannot directly import the Virtual Machines from the source server, the export and import method is also available in Hyper-V 3.0. The following steps explain the procedure of exporting a virtual machine from an existing Hyper-V server:

1. Log on to the source Hyper-V server. Open **Hyper-V Manager** console.

2. Shutdown the Hyper-V guest server.

3. From the **Virtual Machines** column, select the virtual server you want to export.

4. From the **Action** pane, select **Export**.

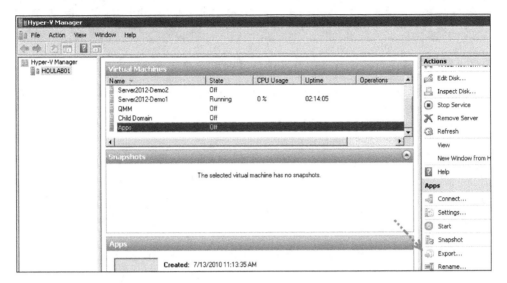

5. In the **Export path** window, enter the location for the export file. Click on **Export**.

6. This process will generate an export (`.exp`) file which can be used to import virtual machines into the target Windows Server 2012 Hyper-V server.

7. The import process is the same as mentioned previously in this recipe.

8. Turn on the target guest machine and verify the settings.

How it works...

Depending on the network configuration, you may need to reconfigure the network settings for the new virtual server. Repeat the same procedure for the other virtual machines on the network to complete the migration.

There's more...

If you are using VMWare, the Microsoft Virtual Machine Converter can be used to convert VMware servers into Hyper-V format. It is a standalone application and can convert the entire virtual machine, which includes the following:

- ▶ Disk
- ▶ Network
- ▶ Configuration
- ▶ Memory
- ▶ Processor details, and so on

Decommissioning old domain controllers (Must know)

Before you can decommission the old domain controllers, you will need to make sure that no other servers or equipment are statically configured to use this server as the DNS server. If so, the DNS IP address needs to be updated with the IP address of the new Windows Server 2012 Domain Controller. The DCPROMO command can be used to remove the existing domain controllers from Active Directory.

How to do it...

1. Log on to the existing domain controller. From the **Run** window, type DCPROMO.
2. Click on **Next** on the **Welcome to the Active Directory Domain Services Installation Wizard** page.
3. If the domain controller is a Global Catalog server, a warning message will appear. Click on **OK**.
4. In the **Delete the Domain** window, click on **Next**. Do NOT select the **Last Domain Controller in the Domain** option.
5. Click on **Next** on the **Remove DNS Delegation** window.
6. It will prompt you for administrative credentials to remove the DNS delegation.
7. In the **Summary** window, click on **Next** to continue the domain controller demotion process.
8. In the **Completing the Active Directory Domain Services Installation Wizard** window, click on **Finish**.

How it works...

After the reboot, this server will be a member server in the Active Directory domain. The Active Directory Domain Services role can be uninstalled from this server at this point. The failed or orphaned domain controllers should be removed from the Active Directory database using the **NTDSUtil** utility. This process is called **metadata cleanup**.

Forest and domain functional level (Must know)

You need to understand the role of the forest and domain functional levels before it can be raised. Some of the new features will only be available when the forest or domain functional level is set to a certain state. For example, in Windows Server 2012, the Dynamic Access Control is only available when the domain functional level is set to Windows Server 2012.

Also keep in mind that, after you configure the forest or domain function level to a certain value, you will not be able to revert it. There are some exceptions to this rule. If the Recycle Bin is not enabled, you can lower the forest functional level from Windows Server 2012 to Windows Server 2008 R2 or Windows Server 2008.

At this point, we have only Windows Server 2012 Domain Controller in the environment and I am not planning to add any down level domain controllers. So we can raise the domain and forest functional level to Windows Server 2012. The pre-Windows Server 2012 Domain Controllers cannot be added in Windows Server 2012 domain functional mode.

The functional level can be lowered by using the `Set-AdForestMode` PowerShell cmdlet. For example, the `Set-AdForestMode -identity domain.com -forestmode WindowsServer2008R2Forest` cmdlets lowers the forest functional level to Windows Server 2008 R2 and the `Set-AdForestMode -identity domain.com -domainmode WindowsServer2008R2Domain` cmdlet lowers the domain functional level to Windows Server 2008 R2.

How to do it...

The following procedure can be used to raise the domain functional level:

1. Open **Active Directory Domain and Trust** from a Windows Server 2012 server or Windows 8 Remote Administration Tools.

2. Right-click on the domain and select **Raise Domain Functional Level...** option.

3. In the **Select an available domain functional level** window, select **Windows Server 2012** and click on **Raise**.

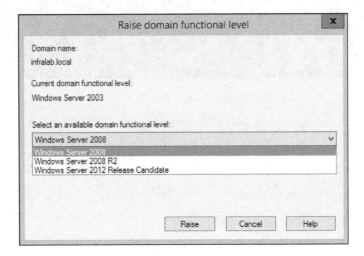

The following procedure can be used to raise the forest functional level

1. Open **Active Directory Domain and Trust** from a Windows Server 2012 server or Windows 8 Remote Administration Tools.

2. From the **Active Directory Domain and Trust** console, right-click on the **Active Directory Domain and Trust** node and select **Raise Forest Functional Level**.

3. In the **Select an available forest functional level** window, select **Windows Server 2012** and then click on **Raise**.

How it works...

In the background, the Active Directory Domain Trust console changes the `msDS-Behavior-Version` attribute value. The `msDS-Behavior-Version` attribute controls which version of operating system can run on a domain controller within the forest and domain. The `msDS-Behavior-Version` value is 5 for Windows Server 2012.

There's more...

Here is an example to verify the value of the `msDS-Behavior-Version` attribute using the `dsquery` command:

▶ To identify forest functional level:

```
dsquery * CN=Partitions,CN=Configuration,DC=domain,DC=com -scope
base -attr msDS-Behavior-Version
```

▶ To identify domain functional level:

```
dsquery * DC=domain,DC=com -scope base -attr msDS-Behavior-Version
```

```
C:\>dsquery * cn=partitions,cn=configuration,dc=infralab,dc=local -scope base -a
ttr msDS-Behavior-Version
  msDS-Behavior-Version
  5

C:\>dsquery * dc=infralab,dc=local -scope base -attr msDS-Behavior-Version
  msDS-Behavior-Version
  5
```

 **Thank you for buying**
Instant Migration from Windows Server 2008 and 2008 R2 to 2012 How-to

About Packt Publishing

Packt, pronounced 'packed', published its first book "*Mastering phpMyAdmin for Effective MySQL Management*" in April 2004 and subsequently continued to specialize in publishing highly focused books on specific technologies and solutions.

Our books and publications share the experiences of your fellow IT professionals in adapting and customizing today's systems, applications, and frameworks. Our solution based books give you the knowledge and power to customize the software and technologies you're using to get the job done. Packt books are more specific and less general than the IT books you have seen in the past. Our unique business model allows us to bring you more focused information, giving you more of what you need to know, and less of what you don't.

Packt is a modern, yet unique publishing company, which focuses on producing quality, cutting-edge books for communities of developers, administrators, and newbies alike. For more information, please visit our website: www.packtpub.com.

Writing for Packt

We welcome all inquiries from people who are interested in authoring. Book proposals should be sent to author@packtpub.com. If your book idea is still at an early stage and you would like to discuss it first before writing a formal book proposal, contact us; one of our commissioning editors will get in touch with you.

We're not just looking for published authors; if you have strong technical skills but no writing experience, our experienced editors can help you develop a writing career, or simply get some additional reward for your expertise.

Microsoft Windows Server AppFabric Cookbook

60 recipes for getting the most out of WCF and WF services, including the latest capabilities in AppFabric 1.1 for Windows Server

Foreword by Ron Jacobs, Senior Program Manager, Microsoft Corporation

Hammad Rajjoub
Rick G. Garibay

Microsoft Windows Server AppFabric Cookbook

ISBN: 978-1-84968-418-7   Paperback: 428 pages

60 recipes for getting the most out of WCF and WF services, including the latest capabilites in AppFabric 1.1 for Windows Server

1. Gain a solid understanding of the capabilities provided by Windows Server AppFabric with a pragmatic, hands-on, results-oriented approach with this book and eBook

2. Learn how to apply the WCF and WF skills you already have to make the most of what Windows Server AppFabric has to offer

Windows Server 2012 Hyper-V Cookbook

Over 50 simple but incredibly effective recipes for mastering the administration of Windows Server Hyper-V

Leandro Carvalho

Windows Server 2012 Hyper-V Cookbook

ISBN: 978-1-84968-442-2   Paperback: 304 pages

Over 50 simply but incredibly effective recipes for mastering the administration of Windows Server Hyper-V

1. Take advantage of numerous Hyper-V best practices for administrators

2. Get to grips with migrating virtual machines between servers and old Hyper-V versions, automating tasks with PowerShell, providing a High Availability and Disaster Recovery environment, and much more

3. A practical Cookbook bursting with essential recipes

Please check **www.PacktPub.com** for information on our titles

Kinect for Windows SDK Programming Guide

ISBN: 978-1-84969-238-0   Paperback: 392 pages

Build motion-sensing applications with Microsoft's Kinect for Windows SDK quickly and easily

1. Building application using Kinect for Windows SDK.

2. Covers the Kinect for Windows SDK v1.6

3. A practical step-by-step tutorial to make learning easy for a beginner.

4. A detailed discussion of all the APIs involved and the explanations of their usage in detail

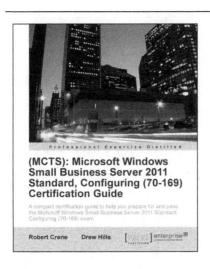

(MCTS): Microsoft Windows Small Business Server 2011 Standard, Configuring (70-169) Certification Guide

ISBN: 978-1-84968-516-0   Paperback: 214 pages

A compact certification guide to help you prepare for and pass the Microsoft Windows Small Business Server 2011 Standard, Configuring (70-169) exam

1. This book and e-book will provide all that you need to know to pass the Microsoft Small Business Server 2011 Standard, Configuring (70-169) exam.

2. Includes a comprehensive set of test questions and answers that will prepare you for the actual exam.

Please check **www.PacktPub.com** for information on our titles